Ordinary/Moving by Penn Kemp

The palimpsest is fading. I have lost
my own memory in contemplating art.

~ Penn Kemp

Ordinary/Moving by Penn Kemp

A Memoir in Verse

Ordinary / Moving

Penn Kemp

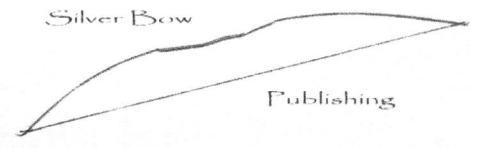

720 –Sixth Street, Box # 5
New Westminster, BC V3C 3C5
CANADA

Title: Ordinary / Moving
Author: Penn Kemp
Cover Art: "Zen Flash" painting by James Kemp
Cover Layout Design: Candice James

All rights reserved including the right to reproduce or translate this book or any portions thereof, in any form except for the use of short passages for review purposes, no part of this book may be reproduced, in part or in whole, or transmitted in any form or by any means, electronically or mechanically, including photocopying, recording, or any information or storage retrieval system without prior permission in writing from the publisher or a license from the Canadian Copyright Collective Agency (Access Copyright)

© Silver Bow Publishing
9781774033517 print
9781774033524 ebook

Library and Archives Canada Cataloguing in Publication

Title: Ordinary / moving / Penn Kemp.
Names: Kemp, Penn, 1944- author
Identifiers: Canadiana (print) 20250165120 | Canadiana (ebook) 20250165198 | ISBN 9781774033517
  (softcover) | ISBN 9781774033524 (Kindle)
Subjects: LCGFT: Poetry. | LCGFT: Autobiographical poetry.
Classification: LCC PS8571.E4485 O75 2025 | DDC C811/.54—dc23

Testimonials

How lovely to see this talented and prolific poet performing at the top of her game at age 80! These are golden poems, brief glimpses of a long life in love and sorrow and art, threaded together with courage and bravado and the kind of gentle Celtic-inspired wisdom we have come to expect in Penn Kemp's work. There are echoes of early Margaret Atwood and late Dorothy Livesay, but transmuted into wide poetic gestures of unusual generosity, empathy, simplicity, community, and kindness.
~Di Brandt, author of *The Sweetest Dance on Earth: New and Selected Poems*

In these strikingly rich poems, Penn Kemp filters her life story as well as that of her family through the lens of ordinary movements. Many-layered, common motions chronicling childhood games such as skipping rope and skating, some movements mastered and others not, are highly relatable to anyone who has failed to Shoot the Duck in skating and been ousted from ballet class. Kemp lives her poetry. Rich in word play, onomatopoeia and metaphor, these poems describe the universal experience of coming of age, finding one's forte, grieving the loss of loved ones and finely balancing family dynamics. Kemp's uncanny juxtapositions reveal her particular genius and wry wit: down the classical halls of Latin and Linnaeus in "A Convoluted Etymology of the Course Not Taken", playing on Frost's poem "The Road Not Taken".

Kemp's favour to her father, gessoing his blank canvases, becomes a poetic manifesto where she waits for words to arise on blank white paper with their own character and personality/ ready to burst off the page and into life. ("Translation"). Divided in to five parts, the poems carry the reader on a familial, compassionate, heartwarming and heartrending journey through life as we move through our own. The eponymous final poem, "Ordinary. Moving" with its subtle wordplay, completes the lifespan into an ongoing motion that encapsulates what all of us seekers desire: ~ **Katerina Fretwell, author of *'Holy in My Nature'* and *'Familiar and Forgiveness'***.

Ordinary/Moving by Penn Kemp

CONTENTS

ORDINARY MOVING
A Memoir in Verse / 11

Part One

Catch as Catch Can / 15
When Rules Change, Roles Follow / 16
When Ideal Meets a Bar / 17
Shooting the Duck / 18
Magnitude Four / 19
One Concession to Go / 20
Ignoring Anatomy / 22
Translation / 23
When Dignitaries Visit / 24
Copper Penny / 25
Drawing Conclusions, Grade Nine / 26
The Race / 27
Joining the Joy-Ride / 29
A Convoluted Etymology of the Course Not Taken / 30
Hiding in Plain Sight / 31

Part Two

Concept of Conception / 35
All Hallow's / 36
The Law of Sevens / 39
Christmas at the Equator, 1979 / 40
Circling the Gulf: A Gain A Loss, Ingrained / 41

Part Three

Over the Marsh and Far Away / 45

Part Four

Along the Line / 55
Belief / 56
Her Orbit of Ellipsis / 57
Silicon Valley / 58

Part Five

Wilder Elder / 61
Play the Game / 62
Ordinary. Moving / 63

Works by Penn Kemp / 65
About Penn Kemp / 67
Acknowledgments / 69

Ordinary/Moving by Penn Kemp

ORDINARY / MOVING

A Memoir in Verse

Perceptions from early childhood are for me best expressed in poetry: our senses are so acute then and the imagery intense. A child's perspective fascinates me as it is still original, unencumbered as yet by expectation. My life began during World War Two and carried on throughout the staid Fifties into those (in)famous Sixties.

The London Ontario artistic scene when I grew up was an exciting foment of new ideas. My father, an abstract painter, was very involved so art was my milieu. Adjusting to social mores at school was something else. My poems present that trajectory: articulating the momentous shifts in consciousness that all those decades offered.

Raising kids in the Seventies, then skipping on to my own Seventies, while grandchildren grow, I can only stand back now to ponder the cycles, patterns of change: what remains and what goes.

~ Penn Kemp

Ordinary/Moving by Penn Kemp

Part One

Ordinary/Moving by Penn Kemp

Catch as Catch Can

London Ont., circa 1950

We tossed a ball against the wall
in sequence, without stopping, following
certain actions and chanting.

Ordinary, Moving
Laughies
Talkies
One hand, the other hand
One foot, the other foot
Front clap, back clap
Front and back
Back and front
Under she goes
Curtsy Salute-sy
Cross your heart
And away she goes

A competitive game played with
pals or practiced alone. Girls only.
Boys would not deign to join us.
When you missed, you were OUT
till your turn rolled 'round again
with the ball, red, white and blue.

When Rules Change, Roles Follow

My first mantra was gleaned from a comic—
    "Poof poof piffles,
make me just as small as Sniffles."

    This spell I claim for mine.

All I need do is sprinkle magic sand
and cross my fingers to join my friend familiar,
a cute and chatty wee rodent called Sniffles.

Mouse size, Mary Jane confronts the family pet,
her formerly cuddlesome calico cat,
now a voracious monster and fearsome hunter
who bears down on her and Sniffles,
gleam intent in globe-green eyes.

Through tree-high stalks of grass,
Cat relentlessly stalks his new prey.
    Evasive, elusive.
  Mary Jane weaves her way
between green shoots of grass,
    the forest she hides in,
precarious shelter to her small self.

Does she recall the formula to shoot herself
back to girl size in time to escape cat's paws
that would pin her between claws to earth?

I am determined to join Mary Jane and her familiar
on far adventures, knowing a comic by its end
would always see us safely home.

When Ideal Meets a Bar

A ballerina whirls in her music box
to the tin tinkle of old Tchaikovsky
whenever I lift the lid.
Whether or not she continues to twirl
as the lid closes is up to conjecture
and the cat in Schrödinger's thought experiment—
spinning incessantly inside as if impatient
for her Prince to lift the glass casket lid
and kiss her free from her coffin.

> Paradox on demand or not,
>   ongoing nonetheless.

At the bar, my satin-coated feet erect
en pointe, pink crimsoned with effort—
as though practice could make perfect
on these swollen, broken, bloody toes.

Stand on one foot. Now the other foot.
But at eight, my feet are declared too big.
Kicked out of class, I dream svelte instead
and breathe the pink of elephants in tutu.

Shooting the Duck

During the snowy winter of 1952 when I was eight
mom drove me each week to the arena
for a figure skating class. She outfitted me just right,
in a navy-blue velvet skirt that barely covered my bum,
a white rabbit muff that kept hands warm,
and a stylish pompom wool cap.

En route mom told me romances of skating to Silver.
But those nasty nicks on the skate blades
would trip me up just as I pushed forward.
Even when I learned not to topple,
I could never figure out just how to shoot that darn duck.
The idea was to hunker down till you
were nearly seated on your skates, then dart one leg out
like the barrel of a gun as you coasted along the ice.

Front clap. Back clap. Front and back. Oops-a-daisy—
Not me. Invariably, I'd end up on my bottom,
gangly colt legs galumphing out in front of me.

That older girl skated graceful rings around those fallen
and splayed in swirls of perfection as, glumly shivering, we
tried to imitate her glide. Like unwelcome, embarrassed dogs,
wet wool legging stench slunk into the arena's crisp air.

But I'd been given a dime and a nickel—my reward after
class was this soggily-savoured cone of chips, best chips
ever! A paper cone soaked in salted vinegar, well worth
taking mittens off for and enduring mom's encouragement
on the red-cheeked ride home.

She'd been an avid skater on outdoor ponds
and still had unwarranted hopes for me.
Nope. Her dream of Winter Olympic Champion held no sway.
Front Clap. Back Clap. Back and front. Front and back.

Magnitude Four

October, 1954

Slam dunk. Hunker down
beneath your little wooden desk
for Hazel, hurricane of the decade.
Beware dipping your hair in the inkwell.
Fear does not further.
Tweedles (roll hands in a tumbling motion)
*Twaddle*s (roll hands in reverse)
Do not suck your thumb
or Miss Morgan will dunk it in an inkwell.
And you will walk home ashamed,
hiding that purple thumb in pocket.

There, there. Hear, hear. Hush now.
Ear to hear while the going's good.
There's no eye to this storm.
Just ear, Right here. Right as rain.
Rain go away. Come again another day
some other way.

Don't hit your head on the desk above you.
Remain still, stationary.
Ordinary means standstill,
nary a move. Barely breathing.

Hold on. Hold to. Hold up. Hold fast
unfastened for goodness' sake
for seatbelts weren't invented yet
and this wild wind might just
carry you off to Oz on its back on a whim,
or on a whirling wind tour of another world.

One Concession to Go

On walking a literal mile to school and back

When Peter jumped and strode me despite a struggle,
he washed my face in snow with a rough leather mitt.
Taking his own sweet time, he backed off, grinning
at my white mask in triumph—his piece of art, his conquest.

"Oh, he likes you," crowed the girls as if in a chorus
from *Carousel*—Billy the bad carnival barker.

Blindly I scrambled ungainly to my feet.
Snow crystals stuck my eyelids shut.
Cheeks scrubbed to flame and fired
with humiliation and fury
and some wild foreshadow of desire
in the heavy tangle of limbs,
him on top in a play of power.

Not fair! I saw red but could not tell
or I'd be told off as a tattle-tale and/or sissy.
The grim code of silence held me frozen all winter
for half a century, as coldly complicit as snow.

My father's father was a champion middleweight boxer.
To head off our street bullies, big boys like Peter Puck,
my dad taught me how to box. I can really throw a punch,
an unexpected left hook beyond what my arm reaches.

My first hit landed in the bully's stomach.
Instantly, he threw up his half-digested lunch
all over his Oxfords.

No-one threw stone-filled snowballs at me on our long walk
through No Man's Land to our two-room school ever again.*

Ordinary/Moving by Penn Kemp

No one would have her face wiped in snow any more.
I could tread safely the cold country mile to cloakroom,
line up at the Girls' door well before the brass bell rang,
late boys left out cold to the strap.

Smugly, I'd pull down those hated leggings mom made me wear,
matted pills of dark blue wool, mixed snarls of snow.
Draped on hook, they'd drip until recess.

Shaking my reversible tartan skirt till creases aligned,
I would transform into a proper pupil
behind my inkwell desk, attentive again
to the daily morning exercises
that would carry me back to mind.

The window steamed. Heat blasted us
to Geography and fractions, Ancient Egypt
and complacent rows of O's across my scribbler,
until my left arm rubbed to black
what my left had just so scrupulously circled.

Lyrics from the Rodgers & Hammerstein musical Carousel
describe Billy, who hits his wife because he cares, to show he cares.
Just so. Yep. Back then.

Ignoring Anatomy

I grew up with art all around. My father,
a painter, gave me some lessons
as I had a quick facility for drawing cartoons.
But I was not interested in form.
He wanted to teach me skeletal, sculptural aspects of art.
I preferred a swift and easy sweep of brush.

Though he was an abstract artist,
he believed in learning basic craftsmanship.
As the critic in him was too strong, I switched to writing
where I could dictate visual perception into diaries
hidden from his eye, his standards.
I could dismiss the importance of appearance.

Dad set me drawing a yellow enamel lamp.
I objected—too mundane. Why recreate on paper
what was plain to see stuck out front?
I'd rather be drawing princesses in damask gowns,
flowing lines full of pinks, swirls, folds,
and nothing inside, no firm form to follow.

Without skeleton, they were mere drapery
but what did I want with bone? No, thanks.
Give me free-floating movement, no body beneath
to stop the course of what I didn't know,
what might magically appear without precedent.

I'd go for the energy pattern, the resonance.
My father and the page have disappeared
but the yellow lamp lights my bedside dresser
as reminder, as '*ding an sich*', before I turn it off.

Translation

I used to prime my father's canvasses
by painting them white with gesso
(a binder mixed with chalk and gypsum)
preparing each surface for his acrylics,
for that colour saturation, from pure primaries
and their complement down to muted neutral hue.

Now I wait with paper's white space
until words arise, images in words.
I watch them come into form, specific entities
with their own character and personality
ready to burst off the page into life, still.

When Dignitaries Visit

Several elderly painters in the Group of Seven
came to my parents' parties. Dad, a practical joker,
had me, at ten-years-old, serve them cocktails
and for nibblies, chocolate-covered grasshoppers,
identity undisclosed until my tray was empty.

No-one asked for seconds but the rush was on
to fill those empty glasses in a flurry of coughs
I feared would kill them.

In the Fifties, they'd be in their Seventies,
ancient and frail as crickets.

London Ont., 1954-5

Copper Penny

If it were juice, a light cranberry tinged with grape.
If wine, a sauterne, a bubbling rosé.
If essential oil neroli, the taste of tangerine.
If scent, what the wind carries from May blossoms,
hawthorn and lilac, lily-of-the-valley intermingled.

A confusion of delight ripe and ready to turn
from cinnamon to ash-grey.

A vibration beyond ultra-violet, where illusions
of colour, shape, ginger to rainbow glints
      among fading memories
strawberry blonde aging well to white.

My grade seven teacher, Miss Morgan, told me
years later that she would sit me in the window
aisle so she could enjoy sun shining on my hair.

Senses interpret synesthesia as taste or scent—
auburn, chestnut, carrot, scarlet, flame.

        Hey, Red!
    Gobbling up youth,
inhaling seven decades past.

Drawing Conclusions, Grade Nine

In our first Science class, the teacher instructed us
to bring, next day, a drawing of the beaker of water
and retort stand he'd set up on his desk.

I knew a still life when I saw one.

As I inherited some skill from my father, a painter,
my pencil sketched and shaded the objects with artful nuance.
My composition displayed a proper balance of proportion and form.

The teacher chose two drawings to illustrate his point.
One was mine, of course, chosen for its beauty.
The other was a clumsy, childish depiction
of the cup in three straight lines.
The water inside, my new classmate had drawn
as simple horizontal dashes.

I shuddered at the scorn the teacher would display.
Poor dear, and she, the daughter of a math professor.

You've guessed the end of the story,
the end of an illustrious science career.

Holding my drawing aloft for all to sneer along,
the man mocked its still-born life.

Right salute. Left salute.

The Race

We've finished Phys. Ed class, running
with the fast boys along a cinder track
behind our school, stalling for time
over undone sneakers, changing out of
awful red and white bloomers
in school colours,
the new stink of sweat still with us
as we while away a Grade Nine
June afternoon on the slope.

Circle skirts we'd hemmed only this morning,
spread over the green.
We're giggling at the word *nipple* pleated
by stray finger nipped.
Peyton Place, page folded down
to mark all proper passages
improperly fingered.

Black dots and cheeks blush
with odd impulses to sink into the hill
or dash into the beechwood,
transformed to dryad or Daphne.

Would that not be safer than this new subtle urge
to chase the other, he whose strong-arm muscles so entice?
Ink marks on a page elicit blush and flush
the errant flicker pulsing down where the body forks,
as yet unknown country.

The skirt,
huge purple flowers on white ground,
encircling pattern to promise arms' embrace,
summer and Grade Ten sock hops.
Magic Moments played over and over,
then *Breaking Up Is Hard to Do*,
undone, unzipped, unseen.

Ordinary/Moving by Penn Kemp

We gyrate to the Twist,
learnt by rolling bath towels behind our backs,
suddenly alert to this new dance,
a competitive sport among those
we thought were best friends forever.

Cross your heart and hope.
While holding your skirt hem up,
slap your knee and toss.

Joining the Joy-Ride

Twirl around all the way after lobbing
and then catch the ball, I dare you.
In my day, any mention of Donnellys
was shunned at Medway High School,
which vigilante descendants attended.

But who could resist on Hallowe'en
heading out in a convertible jalopy
on a joy ride along the Roman Line
to St. Patrick's Church cemetery?

We recited a rollicking poem memorized
in class—matching the bounce over gravel.

*The wind was a torrent of darkness
among the gusty trees.
The moon was a ghostly galleon
tossed upon cloudy seas.
The road was a ribbon of moonlight
over the purple moor—*

And there—under heavy balsam fir branches,
under the round moon glare—the
tombstone of tall pink granite—
a scarlet inscription read—
Murdered. Murdered. Murdered.
We turned and ran back to the car
while the wind whooshed.

*And still of a winter's night, they say,
when the wind is in the trees...
A highwayman comes riding—
      Riding—riding—
A highwayman comes riding,*
along the old Roman Line.

Hiding in Plain Sight

"In case of nuclear threat,
 duck beneath your seat", so the pamphlet reads.

If the bomb goes off (or rather, when)
where shall the family meet?

We plan escape routes out of town,
beyond the fall-out zone.
As if we could hunker down for the accident
off the Bay of Pigs that never came—
or maybe it is still in slow progress,
a procession from stateless ports.

State your aim. Aim your state.
Arm while you're at it.
Or else it's gonna be a wild ride.

So far, so slow but speeding exponentially.
    Moving—wiggle your bum
and catch the ball's bounce off the wall,
counting to the incantatory rhythm.

    Laughies
while not ever allowed to grin.

A Convoluted Etymology of the Course Not Taken

Physics was fun in Grade Ten. A neat balance,
how the atom and its nucleus exactly mirrored
a planet revolving around the sun.
How white refracted into primary spectrum
of Newton's glory. How water was distilled
through the sheer beauty of glass.
How amber made cat's fur fly
and as my favourite jewel, encased ancient tales.

Yes, we had to dissect a frog, desiccating brown leather
despite the formaldehyde, its last swimming hole.
But handsome Jack, my lab mate, sliced it through for parts,
shielding the sight with his broad back
so all I had to ponder was his greased ducktail—
the way certain dark hairs escaped their coil
and small curls lined his neck.

His clever fingers skewered the frog from its skin.
The nape of my neck prickled goosebumps.
Sensation rippled my skin. *Under she goes.*
Theory intrigued me though problems and proof
seemed elusively unnecessary.
Such narrow, restrictive linearity fenced off
further possibility with a single right answer.

When Mr. Jarvis asked me what I wanted to be
      (he knew girls were capable
        of asking the moon these days),
I first chose Zoology, given my ongoing fascination
for lily ponds that pulsed an underwater realm
of quivering black tadpoles, turtles and leopard frogs,
their intact skin shimmering green.
And Biology. I'd pursue that too,
down classical halls of Latin and Linnaeus,
since terminology enclosed intricate worlds
lit from within etymology.

Ordinary/Moving by Penn Kemp

How words revealed
their complicated origin down the ages.

Mr. J. pursed his lips to a smirk:
"Well, my dear..." He held his dissecting knife aloft.
"You'd better get used to carving dead pigeons.
It's what we do in Grade Thirteen."

The classroom suddenly swam.
Startled by the eidolon of a pierced dove,
her white breast feathers charged crimson,
I changed schools, took Latin and Languages,
and kept my birdfeeders full.

Around me the rules slowly shifted, one by one.

Follow the sequence of actions at your turn.
Do doubles far from the wall.

Repeat as near as possible.

Part Two

For Amanda and Jake

Ordinary/Moving by Penn Kemp

Concept of Conception

October, 1943

Family lore returns me to Halloween
at the Gaspé Hotel where my mother
happily feasted with my father upon
a salmon so grand it had to be served
on an ironing table covered in linen.

I've always been fondest of salmon.

The curtain closes on the post-nuptial scene
until next day when my father returned
to his tiny Corvette
(tossed about in forty-foot waves)
to hunt that infamous German submarine
haunting the cold Québec coast.

When I arrived nine months later
as a breech who turned herself around
in mom's fifty-four-hour long labour,
my father was out of touch,
spending the Bank Holiday
at the Lord Mayor of London's
      country home,
    shooting grouse.

All Hallow's

We've celebrated Halloween.
We've drunk and danced and
heard a guitar nimbly played.
Midnight after the party close to
the time of year we first met and
time to celebrate Saturday night.

Little trick-or-treaters have long since left for home.
Our masks are back on the wall once more.
I am lying on our double bed
with my husband deep inside me.
Soon he rolls out and off with satisfied groan
now deepening into snore.

But I between these soft sheets do not sleep.
For there before my wide-open eyes,
cumulus clouds collect somewhere
just below the ceiling in another
nearly here dimension from
a Renaissance painting by Raphael
that should properly be hanging now
in the Uffizi, not our suburban flat.

This palimpsest is fading. I have lost
my own memory in contemplating art.

Substitution has set in. Realities clash.
Return, return to that long ago present.
Nearly here, and attempting to get even
nearer. Mind the gap, no loitering allowed.
Between All Saint's eve and All Saints' Day
something new slips in, slips up and under cover.
Between the sheets, a sly slice of future
parachutes down to land here on
fertile common ground, just when nature
is ready to rest in her six months' sleep.

Ordinary/Moving by Penn Kemp

Samhain, summer's end, winter's start,
the Celts called this most magic cusp
when all our dead return to be feasted
and hungry ghosts hover to sip through straws.
The Celts' New Year begins in deepest dark,
with all potentiality present and possible.

Let us scry through obsidian to clear day.
Faeryland doors open on this night.
Any manner of beings can slip through
either way at the birth of a new month, November—
penultimate of this long-stretching year,
nineteen hundred and sixty-nine.
Time has not yet speeded up.

Halloween. I return again and again
to the scene where you descended.
You dropped in from the clouds,
determined cherub, climbed off
the wall of your plaster molding.

Like all the toys who aspire to flesh
and bone, you wanted in... and you
are welcomed with astonishment
though I don't as yet know you.

I'm a quarter of a century old and I've
long been waiting and wanting this
moment fulfilled, this annunciation.

As the clouds roil, as the clouds billow,
they shape themselves into a myriad of
cherubs beaming down, plump-cheeked
toddlers on a roll. Cupids with a gleam
in their eye so intent on getting into this
womb that lies open before them like
a red welcome blanket, a baby blanket,
a gift of life they'd gladly take, why I can't
tell. I can just determine the yearning for
new form, for flesh, for beginning all over.

Clouds roil, clouds tussle. A shake-up in
heaven reveals one dominant shape,
a shape that solidifies into a specific face.

      This cherub is mine as I am his.
He has chosen with the ferocity of a cupid's dart.
          His aim is sure.

He already has my heart and now he enters
my womb, home for the next nine months
(nearly ten to be precise, but who's counting
those long, hot August nights that await me).

The clouds roll back, as on a chateau ceiling
to reveal blue day as new harmonies of light.
Triumphant paeons blare praise to the winds.
Others recede into wisps of might-have-beens
turning to search elsewhere for nests where
they too might burrow. This one has won.
He who is about to be child has descended.
No doubt as to his being. He is the one constant.

I see this child as he would be when
turning two. The wide brow, the fair hair,
the cheeky grin and cunning cupid's bow.

More than that, the roads diverged
and I saw what he might be,
what he might become.

Three roads, three different ways.
I have told my son once he was grown
and had already lived out two of the ways.

But these I cannot divulge to you, reader.
Wombs may gape, clouds may pour, but
the rest is his story to tell.

The Law of Sevens

What comes in sevens?
The phases we know.
Snow White was princess till seven,
then shocked into a forest octave
till she was ready at fourteen
to know her work—to be Queen.

So I tell my children
who are impressed
with being seven!

The weight and roundness of cells,
one cycle complete.

At five, now ten times their age,
I contemplate the changing series
in the divine chaos we live.

The number seven will split us
opening the door to the world.

But they, my dears,
starting all over again, whistle away
as we do the round of beds and plates,
one for every dwarf and each of us.

Christmas at the Equator, 1979

In the dry air of Quito, low moans drawn
below resonance attract us to the old zoo.

Two giant sea turtles rise above the dust
of their open-air pen. The female squats

half buried in leaves, mouth agape while
the male humps, clacking shells, over and

over her, bellowing as if to call his fellows
five hundred miles east and two miles down

to sea level over on their Galapagos Island.
Newlyweds giggle by in wedding clothes.

My tow-headed children point in wonder at
two turtle tongues wagging like bell clackers.

Circling the Gulf: A Gain A Loss, Ingrained

Signs proliferate as we pass by.
Plastered on the auto dealership plate glass:
SAVE THOU SANDS SAVE THOU SANDS.
Save thou souls, save thy soul,
grain of sand, rain of rant, cycles of want and plenty.

We are so defined by the stories we tell
and those we as children hear.
For years, as I was growing up,
'war stories' were served with dessert at the table.

Over and over, I listened to my grandfather's tale
of leading a regiment of Iroquois troops in battle
on the killing grounds of France.

This warrior tradition emerged in my son
in a fantastical, twisted way.

As a child, he had listened to my father's stories
about his work as a bomb disposal expert
in Scotland during the Second World War.

That stress internalized by my son with dreadful accuracy.
I believe this literalization of memory occurs
down the generations all the time.

Our work is to stop the war in art and in life
so children don't continue to enact conflict.

Ordinary/Moving by Penn Kemp

Part Three

For Heather

Ordinary/Moving by Penn Kemp

Over the Marsh and Far Away

The moon is tangled in the bog. She is lost
and drowning, hair caught, net-tangled.
She will not reappear.
A Marsh Wren sputters, a Bittern startles.
The Great Blue Heron lopes off slowly, alone.
Does she rise with them, a bubbling cry from
what was gut or heart, who can say when
words desert, when she leaves
beauty abruptly behind.
She follows the false fairy-fire, green
foxfire further beyond any known path.
Morass blurs.

Shorn, she moves through the elements
more surely now.
The persistent life of a breath passed
away in what might have been just
a passing phase if only she'd kept on. Going.
Only a girl. Still only a girl. Only a girl forever.

Just a child
who now
never ever
will be grown.
She who
would
       not
harm a fly
suicided

So decided a
       step
daughter
       collided
with the law of
levity and
       lost

out
      on a limb
or in
limbo
love for
love for
lorn

Grief is no time for
emotion. Grief is no
time. Grief is no
thing. Not a thing.
Knotted.
Wring your hands in
vain. *In vanitas*
blame.
Wring your hands inside
out. Rip your rings off.
What could you do. What
could you have done.
What more could you have
done. It is done.

What is lost cannot now
be found. Can only be
remembered.
            But we know
memory is faulty.
Memory falters. Memory
fails.
We search for clues in
the past.
            Red clues,
led by Ariadne
through a labyrinth of
our own
making.
What minotaur might
linger in the dark
centre?

So many glimpses
flicker, a shining
face, aged four.
A sullen face, aged
twelve.

If only we could
re/member
what might have
been.
If only the shards
would fit together.
If only we might
recall what would
cause such

On /off /on / off
Lights glimmer
Is that you?
Are you there?
I can sort
of feel
her here.
Can you?
As if we
could call her
back, call her on
to continue
on.
Hope faints.
 Hope is less.

I wish hope would
feign difference but
hope, you are false.
Out come out
wherever you are.
What do you expect?
You are less.

Careful what you wish
for. After long absence –
change. After death.
Change.

Shades fade.
The dead are not really
gone as long as we can
what, imagine them in
a movie, a projection
on screen?
                Begin
the reel again. Reel her
in. Back to the real.
And what is?
How many dimensions
must we skip
over to reach
the intangible, invisible,
Ordinary, moving.
One hand. The other
hand. Knows what?

Did you ever guess?
It never crossed
my mind
less
meandering
more
for goodness'
ache

And you, Sparrow.
Did you hope to be
found in the nick
of time
       less
time
What we call time is
more or less

what we deserve.
Hope is less.

Would you now regret
a moment's lapse, a moment's
fury?
Did you despair a moment
or a decade?
Stupid queries. Stupid because
never to be resolved. A riddle
we'd rather not guess.
A muddle we cannot escape.
We can however
let you go, how
I don't yet
know. No.
Not yet, not
now.
Leaving is best
left to the end
When nothing is
left.

But look
outside
where snow hangs
heavy on the fir.
What for?
What is hiding
among the cattails?
Look up
where grey gives way
to grey.
Cloud covers
over.
Cloud behind
cloud. Cloud
beyond.

        The sky opens and opens unto more sky.

Ordinary/Moving by Penn Kemp

                    Lighter and lighter
she rises. Nothing can bog her down now.
She is ageless, genderless, free from teenage
anguish. Wished free.
        While we age more with each moment,
caught in cultural specifics that label us *he*, *she*, *they*
confined to the particularities of person,
of memory.
                                  Of loss.

She scries how to float above a body
left behind.
Her route is through the Bardo and beyond.
Back in the realm of time, we have just
habit to fall back on. Familiar wet
clothes that suit us to a thread worn
and weary with mourning. Hair pulled
out by the root. *If only.* Only if. Faith
less. Faith full. We don't know which.
She has chosen. Nor why. But words
over the abyss, one by one, a phrase or
sentence, lead us out of the bog, home.

And on the way, perched on the word, we bend
to pick blueberries, sprigs of Labrador tea, scarlet
cranberry. Bog fruit found and offered freely
to whatever guides are willing to hold her flame.

No bittern croaks.
The heron has flown
without a wave,
her secret hidden.
Truth is not so easily
out. Truth lies
in details I spare you.
Under cover.
Soft snow falling.
Soft now melting
upon pond water.

But listen.
What is that whisper
in the dry grass? What wind
blows when none
can be seen?
Or felt.
Is it you there
in the falling
ice crystals?
A distance. Is it
a wisp of breeze?
We haven't a clue.

When the pond erupts
in a bubble you cannot
interpret, do you wish
for difference, what do
you long
for now it is
too late?
Nothing rises
to the surface but
another bubble.
She is long under
water. She is long
gone.

When the bough breaks
do you think there
she is there she well
might be?
When the wind stirs
do you believe she
has breathed out
along
the limb?
"Girl of the Limberlost",
she read
limber
lost

Ordinary/Moving by Penn Kemp

And found,
foolish, giggling
hysterically.
And found
fortune to the quick
And found as
if there were answers.
Foundling.
Foundering.
Fond fare
well, that's not
possible.
Not yet.
And yet.

Who is lost?

Ordinary. Not moving.
Clap at the front
Clap at the back
Front to back
Back to front
Roll hands in a tumbling motion.
Roll hands in reverse.
Wring, wrung. Ring, rung.
For whom. For you.

Do you blame?
Don't go there.
Start again.

Living with our beloved dead,
we move with the light weight
of all we remember. We move
on. We move in. We move
through.
One hand. The other hand.
Gone, gone, completely.

Part Four

For Ula and Kai

Ordinary/Moving by Penn Kemp

Along the Line

Nine-month-old Ula stands
across from her birthplace,
braced almost steady in her playpen,
        and beams
as we circle our bellies in the old way,
simulating birth, calling down ancestor women,
whirling alongside great-grandmother spectres
who recede in the space of one year
and re-appear in the new-born,
in planted memoriam.

We sweep legacy in their wake
among the black-braided women of Tulum.

Ocean rhythm, blue sky on white sand.
Truly croned and crowned grandmother,
we circle the lineage of women—
daughter-to-daughter-to-daughter.

Drawn again by the weight of love
to the spiral dance.

Belief

In the space of a year she has learned to sit,
to stand, to walk, to totter forward in a run.
She has seen one full round of the seasons.
She wraps her family round her little finger.

Now just before dusk we stroll hand in hand
to witness the pelicans' evening beach patrol.
Gliding over the sea in formation, skimming
just overhead, flapping slow time, in synch.

Ula studies the procedure, dropping my hand
to edge forward, neck outstretched, arms aero-
dynamically angled. She flaps and flaps
along the sand, following the pelican's flight,
ready for that sudden lift. Again, again,
    till the last pelican has flown.

        Dragging her heels home,
Ula braces her body against the rising breeze,
bewildered that she too can't take off to sky
but game to try again tomorrow...

Her Orbit of Ellipsis

My granddaughter is going as
Wonder Woman for Halloween.
She's practiced swinging her Lariat of Truth
so I'm reading up on Artemis,
protectress of young girls
and the archetype for
our current Wonder Woman.

Arrow to hand, she alights on the mark,
drawing her bow on intruders.
Artemis herds young *artoi*, girls of eight or so
away from polis, the city, into wilder woods
where she reigns Queen
and they, her willing apprentices,
stay snared till puberty.

Artoi, little Bears,
they follow their Great Bear
into the chase and Orion hides,
the hunter hunted and flung
out to constellation.

My granddaughter
will go trick or treating
and return, gleeful,
with a sack full
of eternal returns.

Silicon Valley

Do you remember the days
when silicon was an element
central to sand, the sense of
grit between your toes by
the river just beyond the
reverberating slap of the old
screen against the door jamb
where wood never quite
met wood and was kept
together by hook in eye?

It was revolutionary then to
discover silicon also sprouted
in the segments of scrawny
horsetail that surrounded
the house as soon as sand
met any sort of soil.

You'd chew the stalk thoughtfully,
its brittle twist into saliva,
thinking dinosaur, this plant
alive at the same time and
huge the way the past is
thrown by a trick of light
projected onto shadow
out of all proportion.

Yourself the size of an ant
in a jungle of horsetail.
And then the thud of approaching
brontosaurus, its jaws dripping
green weeds the size of trees,
its wet eye unable to focus
on anything as small as you
at the age of seven.

Part Five

Ordinary/Moving by Penn Kemp

Wilder Elder

Curtsy Salute-sy
Cross your heart
And away she goes.

Whassup?
Not I! Down again,
but not for the count.

Laid up, lying down
and counting the days
until I can get up again.

A gain, a loss, what's the difference,
but still
Unsettled. Restless.
Twitchy. Agitated.
On edge. Over the edge.
Beyond
Stirring
Whisk
Rouse
Rise
wryly

Play the Game

One foot. The other foot. Each motion opens
to a moment, the poem as glimpse into a life.

We all kill ourselves eventually, inevitably.
My beloved is diabetic but sneaks sweet treats.

My heart is weak but I stress it, taking on 'way
too much. My friend needs a drink on the hour.

Another devours junk food. One more throws
tantrums despite family history of heart failure.

I strain my eyes in editing on screen till holes burn
in my dear maculae. Degeneration all round.

Defenses up. Excuses proliferate.

What 's mine may differ in degree from yours
but not in kind.

Kindness comes first,
comes last for the duration.
Kindness endures. Kindness lasts.

Ordinary / Moving

through the seasonal
cyclic completion
into another
the next
with joy
trepidation
and dread.

We anticipate another
win some, lose some
looking for wisdom

Ordinary/Moving by Penn Kemp

Works by Penn Kemp

Poetry
Lives of Dead Poets; Incrementally; A Baker's Dozen; P.S. (with Sharon Thesen); A Near Memoir; River Revery; Fox Haunts; Local Heroes; Barbaric Cultural Practice; From Dream Sequins; Pinceladas; Re: Animating Animus; Poemas Escolhidos de Penn Kemp/ Selected Poems; C'Loud; Sarasvati Scapes; Gathering Voices; Suite Ancient Egypt; Vocal Braidings; Incrementals; Throo; Eidolons; Some Talk Magic; Travelling Light; Animus; Binding Twine; Toad Tales; Changing Place; Clearing; Tranceform; Bearing Down

Drama
The Triumph of Teresa Harris; The Dream Life of Teresa Harris; What the Ear Hears Last; Angel Makers; The Epic of Toad and Heron

Prose
What Springs to Mind; Four Women; The Universe is One Poem.

Anthologies edited
Poems in Response to Peril (with Richard-Yves Sitoski); Women & Multimedia; Performing Women; Jack Layton: Art in Action; Poem for Peace in Many Voices, Vol. 1 & 2; CVii: Spiritual Poetry in Canada; Twelfth Key; IS 14

Recordings
Incrementally; Helwa! a Sound Opera, Experiencing Ancient Egypt; Night Vision: a Sound Opera; Five Eerie Pieces; Luminous Entrance: a sound opera for climate change action; Memory Vision; Xtra Text/ure: a Sound Opera; Darkness Visible: a Sound Opera; Trance Dance Form: a Sound Opera; Re:ANIMATING ANIMUS: a Sound Opera; Soundspoke: a Sound Opera; Gathering Voices; Time Less Time; Two Lips; Four Women; Melisma; Sarasvati Scapes: a Sound Opera; From the Lunar Plexus: a Sound Opera; From the House of Pan; On Our Own Spoke; Carnivocal: A Celebration of Sound Poetry; Breakfast @ Epiphonemes; Temporary Harmonies; Epiphanies; Inspiritrice; Jamming In The Bardo; Ear Rings; Bearing Down (for four voices)

Ordinary/Moving by Penn Kemp

About Penn Kemp

Penn Kemp has participated in Canadian cultural life for sixty years— writing, editing, and publishing poetry, fiction, and plays. Her first book of poetry, *Bearing Down*, was published by Coach House, 1972, followed the next year by *IS 14*, the first anthology of women's writing in Canada. Penn has since edited a number of anthologies by Canadian writers, starting with *Twelfth Key* in 1976. Most recently, she co-edited *POEMS IN RESPONSE TO PERIL*, raising money for Ukraine. Penn has published 36 books of poetry, prose, and drama, with 7 plays and numerous CDs and DVDs of spoken word produced. Her work explores environmental and feminist concerns, though she is best known as a sound poet. Delighting in multimedia, Penn is active across the web.

Out now is Penn's *Lives of Dead Poets* (above / ground press). Her latest collection of sound poetry, *INCREMENTALLY*, is up on https://www.hempressbooks.com/authors/penn-kemp as e-book and album. See https://riverrevery.ca/. She has been described as a "vibrant, poetic El Niño", and a "one-woman literary industry".

Penn was London, Ontario's inaugural Poet Laureate (2010-13) and Western University's Writer-in-Residence (2009-10). Chosen as the League of Canadian Poets' Spoken Word Artist (2015), she is also a Life Member of the League. For 7 years, she hosted a literary radio show, *Gathering Voices*, featuring local and global artists. Penn has performed her poetry at festivals world-wide, touring in England and Scotland, Germany, India, the U.S. and Brazil, as well as across Canada from 1974 on. She has served as writer-in-residence from Labrador to the Yukon and from Buffalo, New York, to the University of Mumbai and the University of Rondonia in the Amazon. Her "poem for peace for many voices" has been translated into 136 languages, published in two volumes, book and CD, and performed by 3,000 people for World Peace Day. It is deposited in the UN Library and Egypt's Alexandria Library.

Updates: https://www.pennkemp.weebly.com,
http://pennkemp.substack.com and
https://facebook.com/pennkemppoet/.

Ordinary/Moving by Penn Kemp

Notes and Acknowledgements

In memory of beloved Ula, Gavin, and Heather. With gratitude to kind and generous friends who encouraged this writing: gifted writers all.

My thanks to editors everywhere! Several of these poems first appeared elsewhere in earlier versions. See: http://tuckmagazine.com/tag/penn-kemp and https://silverbirchpress.wordpress.com/2016/03/22/a-study-in-red-hair-poem-by-penn-kemp-my-mane-memories-poetry-and-prose-series/. "Belief" was chosen for The League of Canadian Poets' Poem in Your Pocket Day and appears in *Universal Oneness: An Anthology of Magnum Opus Poems from around the World: (360 poems by 360 poets from 60 Countries)*. Special thanks to Andreas Gripp for publishing early versions of some of these poems in my chapbook, *a near memoir: new poems,* and in his new literary magazine, *Sola Poeta,* Issues 1 and 2.

On "Translation": this video was created by the brilliant Dennis Siren with me through the support of London Arts Council and the City of London ON: https://www.youtube.com/watch?v=WMqzgfLJtws.

How exciting to offer Mary McDonald's two poetry films of poems from *Ordinary / Moving*: "Silicon Valley" and "Believe..."! Her animations appear on https://riverrevery.ca. These poetry films have been shown at Museum London for WordsFest.ca; Houston's Reel Poetry Festival; London Public Library; and the Open Educational Resources Conference, Galway, Ireland. Our collaboration was made possible through a City of London Community Arts Investment Program grant.

I'm grateful to the London Arts Council and Ontario Arts Council's Recommender Grants for Writers for time to write *Ordinary / Moving*. Photo of Penny Kemp in 1950: Jim Kemp. I was reading *The Adventures of Tom Sawyer*.

Photo on back cover by Christine Romard.

Ordinary/Moving by Penn Kemp

www.ingramcontent.com/pod-product-compliance
Lightning Source LLC
Chambersburg PA
CBHW052206070526
44585CB00017B/2088